Pull By Magic

By Ken Miller

Published in the UK by
POWERFRESH Limited
21 Rothersthorpe Crescent
Northampton
NN4 8JD

Telephone   0845 130 4565
Facsimile   0845 130 4563
E Mail   info@powerfresh.co.uk

Copyright ' 2003 Ken Miller & Stephen Leslie Designs
Cover and interior layout by Powerfresh

ISBN 1902929500

All rights reserved. No part of this publication may be reproduced or
transmitted in any form or by any means, electronic or mechanical, including
photocopying, recording or any information storage and retrieval system, or for
the source of ideas without the written permission of the publisher.

Printed in Malta by Gutenberg Press Ltd
Powerfresh April 2003

So, What is Pulling?

Pulling is impressing.

It's about standing out from the crowd. It's being noticed. It's having something which says, "This gal or guy is different". Hmm, could be worth watching. Might just be interesting."

Magic *is* interesting.
You're in with a chance.

Kick Start

If you're not known as a magician, how do you get round to showing somebody a trick without having to say, Can I show you a trick? One way is *not* to start with with a trick but with a puzzle. Here's one that's particularly good in a bar or similar situation. It is Ivan Morris' Cherry and Cocktail Challenge from his *Pillow-Book Puzzles*. It's easy when you know how but surprisingly difficult when you don't.

You need four paper clips to make the cocktail glass and a coin to represent the cherry, as shown opposite.

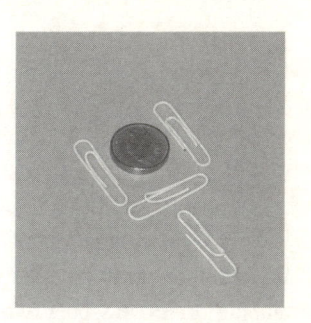

The challenge is to remove the cherry from the glass without touching it, only moving two pieces of the glass and leaving the glass in the same shape as when you started.
Try the puzzle before turning the page. That way you get a good measure of the difficulty (and simplicity!) of the puzzle.

Slide the horizontal clip *halfway* to the right.

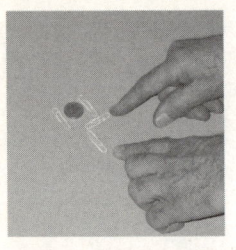

Move the far left clip over to the right to touch the horizontal clip in its new position.

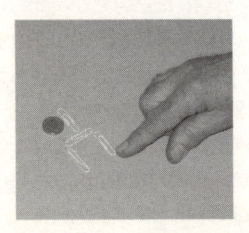

Coin You Guess?

Another good way of starting is with a bar bet. Here's an oldie but goldie that can be done with any coin, British or foreign but, as an example, try it with a pound coin.

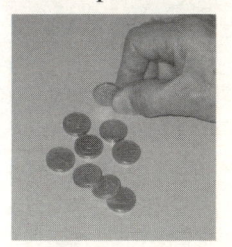

If you stand a pound coin on edge, how many coins would be needed to make a pile to equal its height? Try it, you'll be surprised. *Everybody* guesses less than is needed.

Piggy in the Middle

For another good oldie but goldie lay out 3 coins like this:

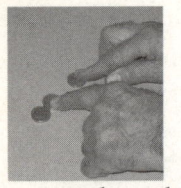

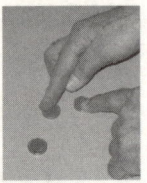

You have to place the coin on the right between the other two without touching the one on the left or moving the one in the middle. Press down on the centre coin with your left forefinger and flick the right-hand coin against it. The impact knocks the two coins apart so you can slide the third coin between them.

Fly Me

Ten fighters flying north but south is where the action is. Three only, flying in straight lines, turn the formation round.
How? (The coins must remain flat on the table.)

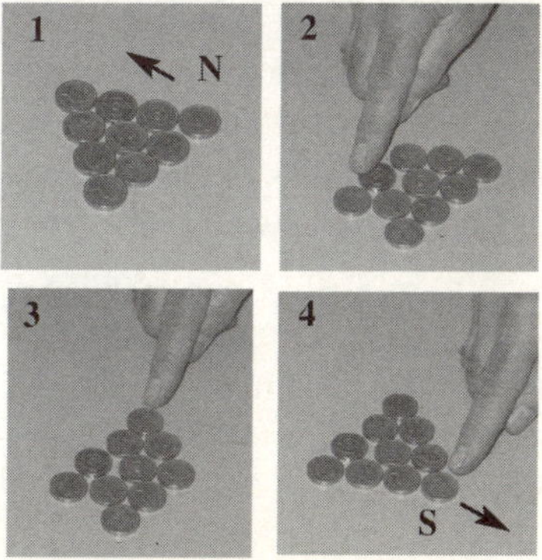

It's Matchic!

Use 12 matches to show what makes a perfect match.

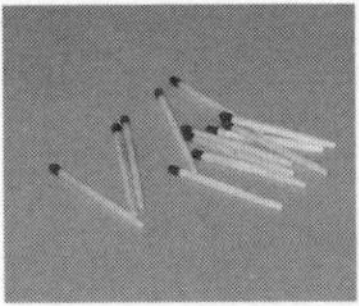

Match puzzles are useful since they can be done with other things like toothpicks, cotton buds, hair or paper clips.

Jest Four Fun

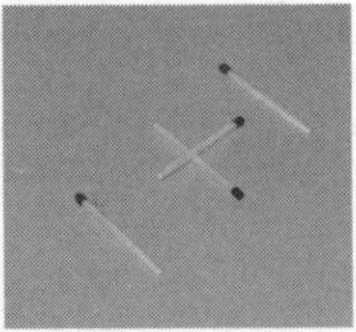

Make four equal two.

Matter thru Matter

First show hands like this. The vertical stick is clipped between the first and second finger tips.

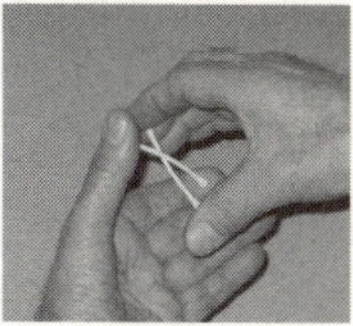

Tap them together then lower the right thumb very slightly so one stick can pass the other.

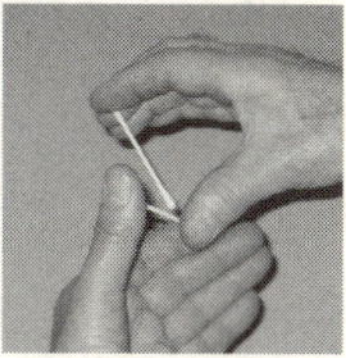

Immediately close the gap.

A Trick of Note

Hand a note to the pullee (for ease of description, I'm going to assume it's a girl if not, adjust accordingly.) "Hmm, interesting hands. Would you hold that for a moment please?"

Take two paper clips and drop them on the table near to her. Look intently at her hands and say, "Yes, very interesting. Thanks, I'll take the note". Fold the note into three.

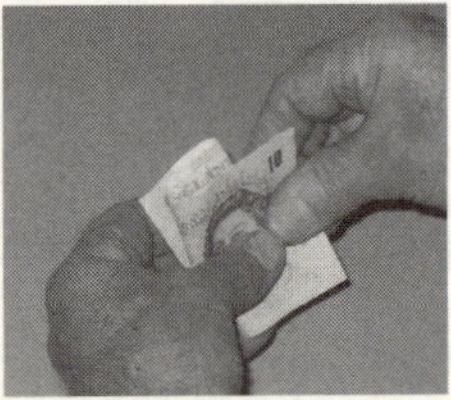

Pick up the clip nearest to you. "Yes, very interesting." Use it to clip the two folds nearest to you together.

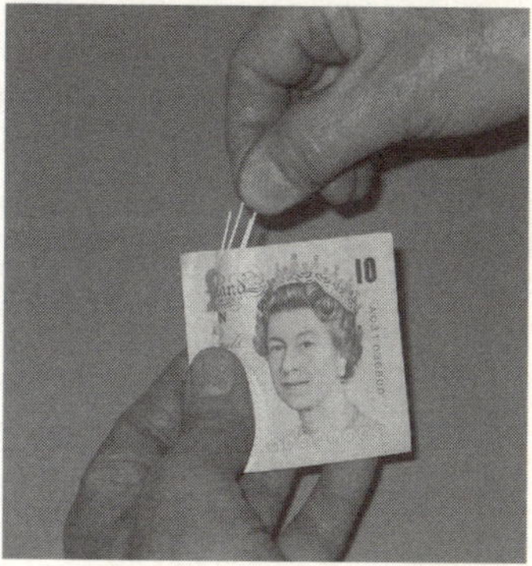

Gesture towards the other clip and say, "Could you pass that one, please? Thanks." Clip the other two folds together.

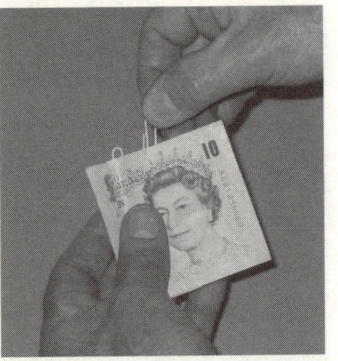

She is now involved in the action: first the note, now a clip. Ice broken, you have got her attention.

Hold the note near her mouth and say, "Would you blow on that, please?" Draw it away from her face and with both hands, pull sharply in opposite directions.

The clips will fly off. Do *not* pick them up. Let *her* discover that they are linked.

You need to prepare for this follow-up by having *another* pair of linked clips (from a previous miracle?) ready, preferably in a right-side pocket. As soon as the clips fly off and attention is on them, *immediately* fold the note in three as before (page 12), Clip the two nearest folds together.

As you say, "I'm not surprised, I said you had unusual hands," take the linked clips from her and clip the other two folds together. As with your pair, one clip does the clipping and the other hangs free. Practise this so you can do it almost without looking so you can deliver your casual line and smile at her.

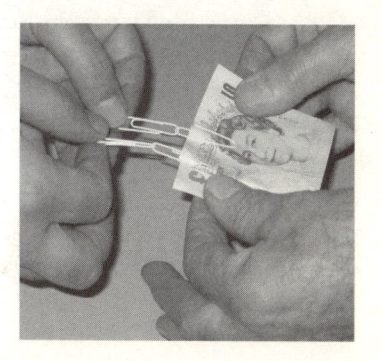

You are now going to do exactly the same thing as before, pull sharply on the note in opposite directions. This is unusual since, normally, one doesn't repeat a trick but in this case it *adds* to the effect. Ask her to take hold of the two 'dangling' clips, one in each hand and hold them very firmly.

Draw her hands away from her face and when you are sure she has a good grip on them say, "Blow!" and pull the note sharply as before. The clips will fly off linking her two hands together, producing a much greater sense of involvement.

"You're obviously good at that."

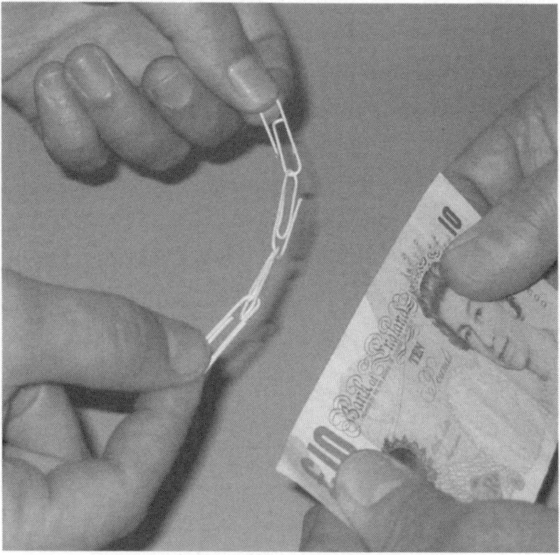

"Oh, you've *definitely* got something going." Make a slight pause. "Maybe we have?" As she is examining the chain of clips put two *sharp* creases into the note at the ends of the Queen's lips and curve the mouth section *inwards*.

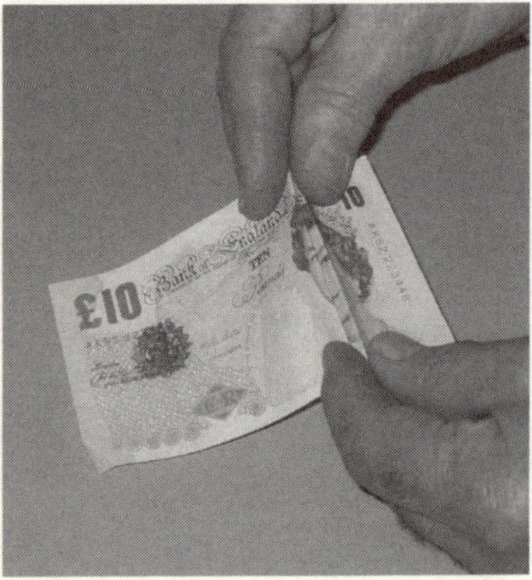

With the Queen *facing the girl,* tilt the note towards you. "Oh, look, even the Queen's smiling. She *must* approve."

Tilt the note in the opposite direction and the smile changes to a frown.

She may not see this immediately but this is all to the good. You will probably be *forced* to lean over her and actually hold her hands so she can see the illusion properly. "Just being helpful".

TIP: Try this in front of a mirror to convince yourself that it actually works and then try it out with different notes including foreign ones, if possible. It is the kind of thing that it is good to encourage other members of the party to try and to show each other.

23

"It's an optical illusions, I love 'em. Do you know this one? It's the same as those Magic Eye books that were all the rage. They're even on the net now. You had to sort of look *through* them to be able to see the effect. Try this. Hold both your hands up in front like this."

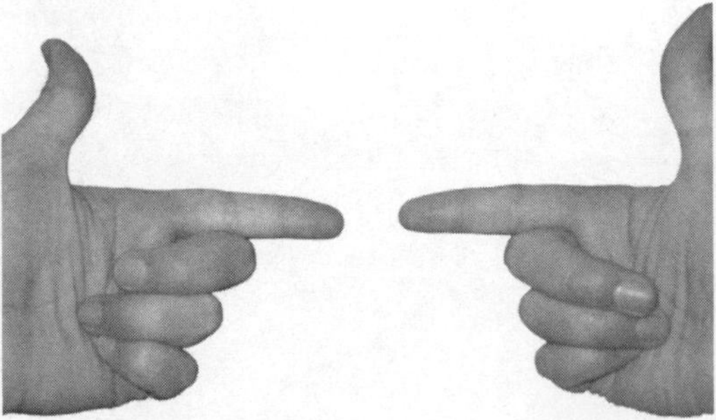

"That's it, fingers slightly apart and in front of your nose."

The correct position is about 20 cm (8") in front of your nose so you may *have* to move her hands. Correction. You will have to move her hands even if they end up in the same position.

"Now *stare* through, between your fingers and focus on the other side of the room. See it?"

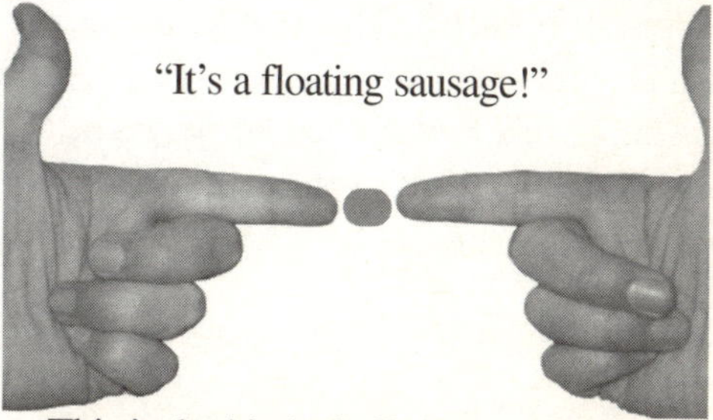

"It's a floating sausage!"

This is the kind of effect that you see.

"They're flying tonight." If in a group, get as many as possible to try it. If somebody says they can't see it, you may want to use a line like, "You've got to be a silly sausage like me." This is the type of line to look at carefully. If it happens to suit *your* personality and the company, fine. If not, not.

If optical illusions and the like interest you, you may want to mug up on them. Just key "Optical Illusions" into Google or another search engine. If you think you've caught her attention, take out a ballpoint and say, "I'll send you one. What's your email?"

Pull out a ballpoint and write it on your palm or a drinks mat. "Cute. I'll send it as an attachment. Could lead to one." www.SandlotScience.com has a link "Greetings Cards" where you can choose an optical illusion and music to go with it. Can make a nice talking point and a great way to make contact. Hold your pen like this:

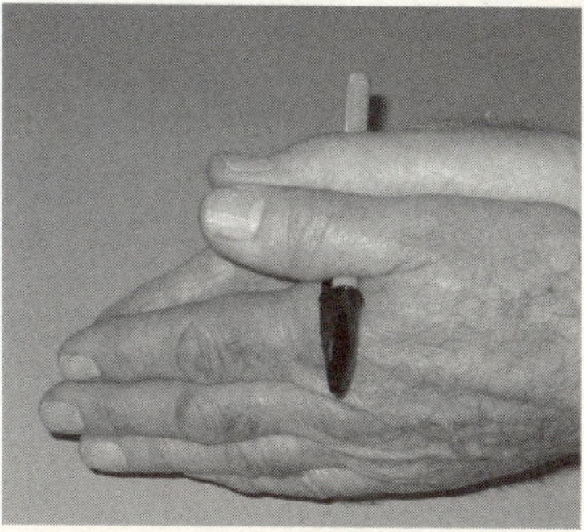

"I'm one of the Secret Seven, you know. It's so secret, I don't know the other six. It's murder getting a quorum. We've got a secret sign. You've got to do it to get into a meeting. It works like this. You've got to start with the pen like this ....."

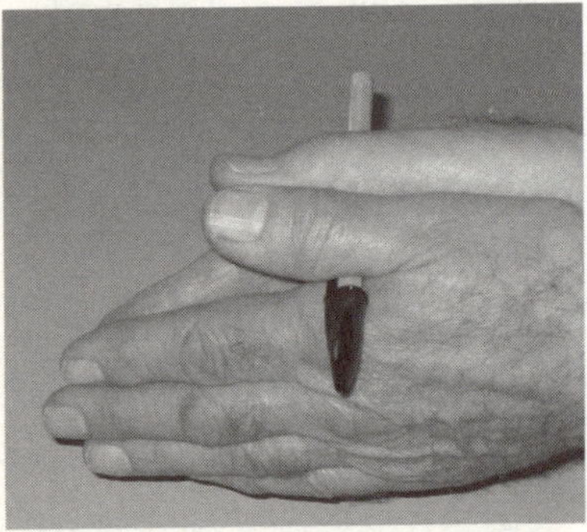

"And finish like this....."

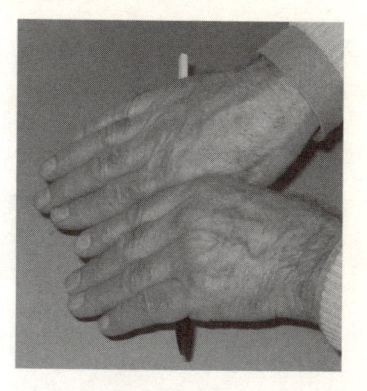

"Without separating your hands. Try it." Again, get as many as possible trying it. It doesn't have to be a pen. For example, at table, get them to try it with the cutlery.

This is how you do it.

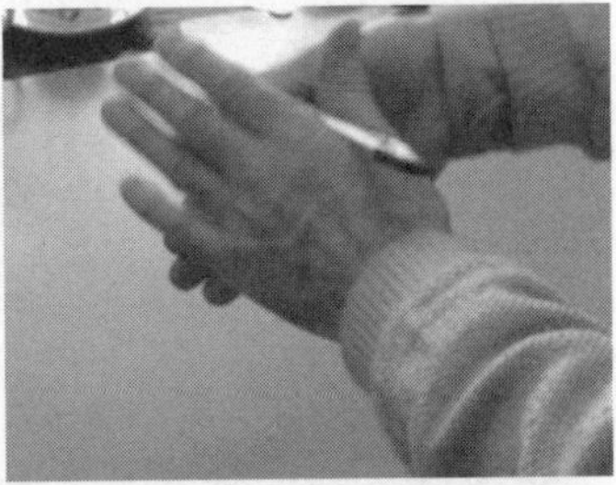

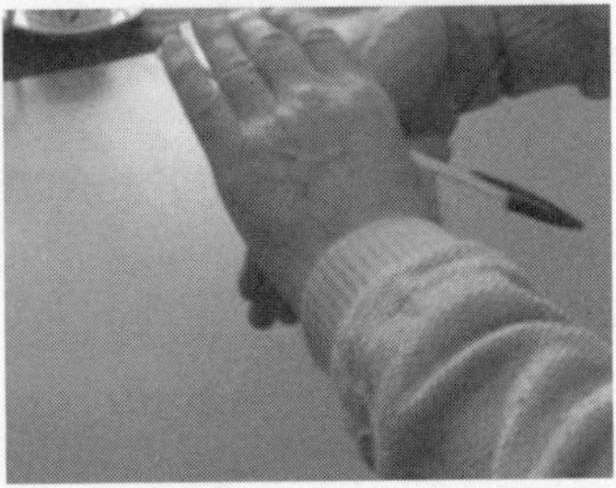

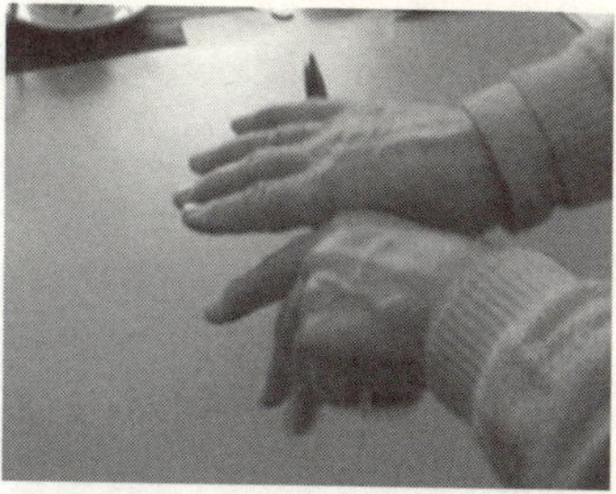

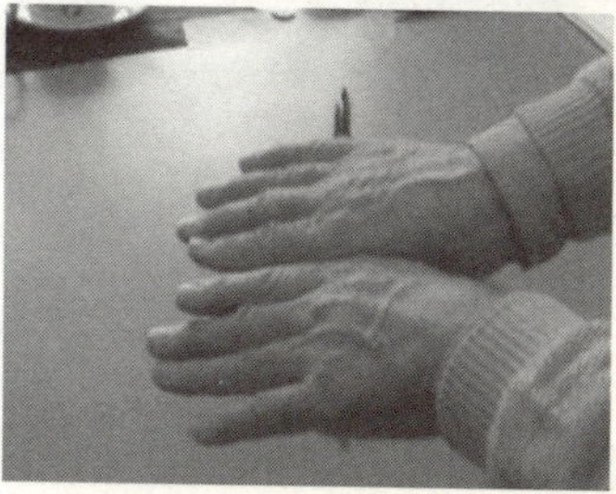

31

Handy Magnet

This is a very old bit of nonsense but worth putting in as a quickie while chatting. "It's easy if you've got a magnet handy. Or a handy magnet."

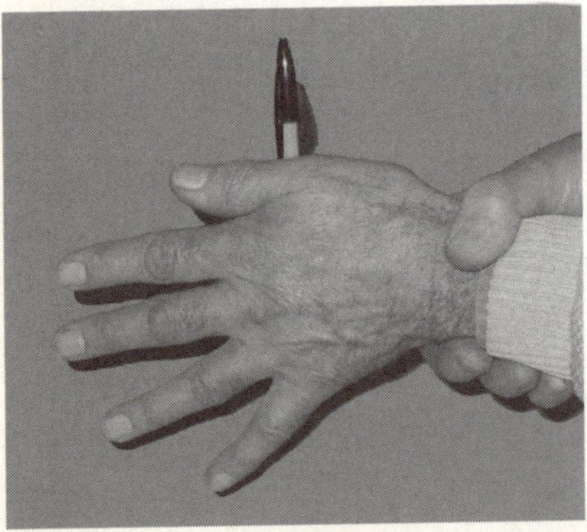

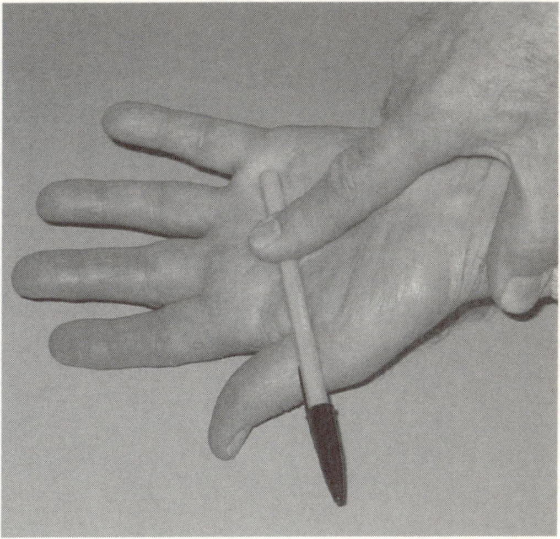

33

Thumbthing Special

At some stage, in this typically informal situation, it is reasonable to "show how it's done" - spend as much or as little time on this as you feel is appropriate. As an opening line to it, say, "Oh, what you need is a removable thumb." Hold out your right hand with its back to your audience and bend the thumb down, at right angles, towards your palm.

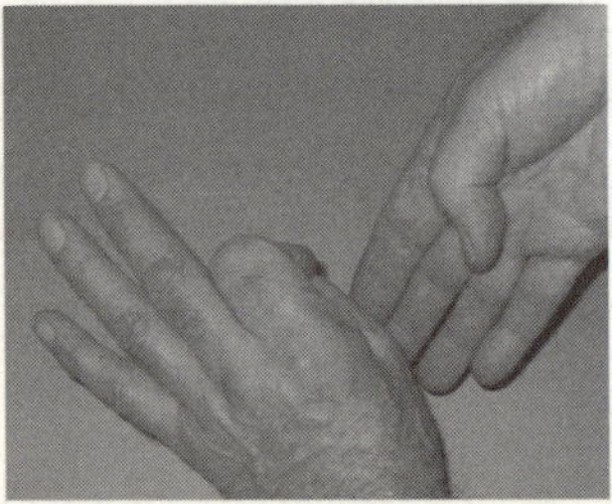

At the same time, bend your left thumb so that it's top half is horizontal and bring your forefinger down on top of if so that it overhangs slightly to the right.

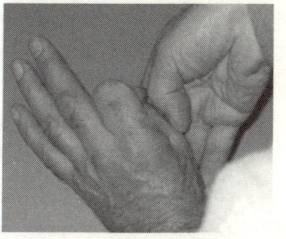

Immediately bring your hands together so that the lower half of your left thumb fits against the bent-down upper half of your right thumb and your left forefinger rests on top, hiding the join. Separate your hands to "remove your thumb," then quickly bring them together.

Nails - No Nails!

"Nails."

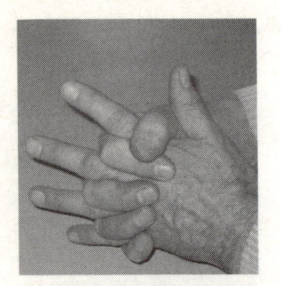

"No nails!"

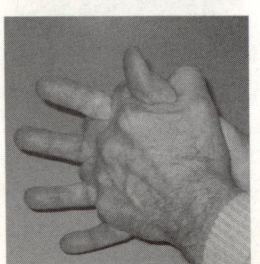

You repeat this a few times, in fact what you are doing is this.

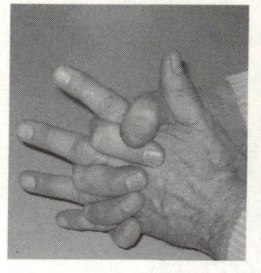

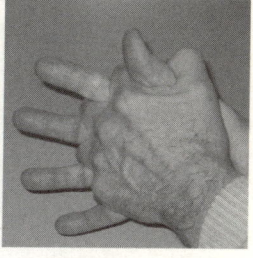

As you turn your wrist, rapidly close your outstretched fingers and extend the clenched ones. The larger turn-over movement conceals the change.

Funny Finger

This is another bit of business that is well worth perfecting, particularly if you suspect she has a younger brother.

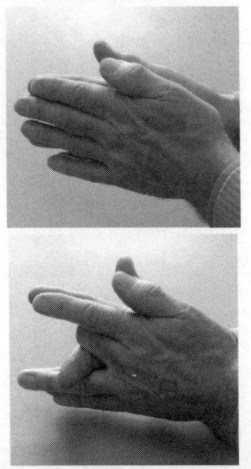

Now swivel your hands in opposite directions.....

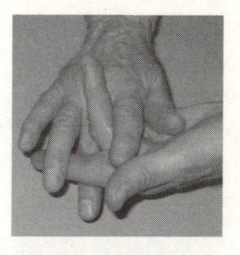

and waggle your fingers!

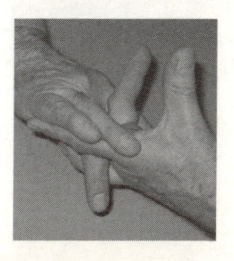

Luv Mug

Pick up her coffee mug like this gripping it between your first and little fingers:

Always check first to make sure that it is not too full or too hot but, in practice, I've never had a problem with this idea.

Say, "Oh, look, a Luv Mug! *Two* handles. Are they trying to tell us something?" Pretend to be going to drink from it but immediately return the mug to the table.

In the same way, you can pick up a tumbler and say, "Me, I prefer a tankard."

Tea Hee!

You can even hold a cup and saucer with one hand and drink from it, leaving your other hand free.

Right thumb presses against the rim of the cup, braced against the 1st and 2nd fingers, 3rd and 4th fingers are well under the saucer supporting it.

Magnetic Personality

"Of course, it helps if you've got a magnetic personality." Hold your ballpoint horizontally, take off the cap and rub it on your sleeve. Grip the very tip of the cap between your thumb and forefinger and hold it just on the end of the pen.

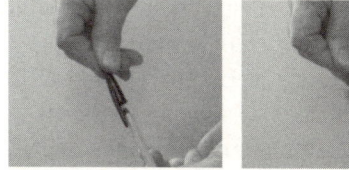

Squeeze the tip of the cap and it will shoot on to the pen. "Look at that! A miracle and at no extra charge. Well ..... electrostatic."

Find the Lager

Find the *Lady* is a well-known racecourse swindle that's still going strong. It makes an excellent talking point and here's how to introduce it. You need three drinks mats that are, if possible, advertising a lager. If not, simply modify your patter slightly. The important point is that opposite sides of the mats should be different in some way.

"Did you see that at Epsom?" (Use local or topical reference,) "Chap was had up for doing the Three card Trick, Find the Lady.

He denied it. Said he wasn't doing Find the Lady, he was doing Find the *Lager!*

"He told the judge it was a proper game of skill, in fact he showed him, You use three mats and the punters see both sides." (Turn them over a couple of times.) "No trickery. Then you lay 'em out like this."

"What you've got to do, Your Honour, is to take three moves to turn them all lager-side up, just like the middle one."

"The judge bends down *slightly*. (Mime) So the Clerk of the Court has to twist himself in a knot to hear him." (Mime) (Very posh voice) "What does the defendant mean by a move?" Clearing his throat, the Clerk pipes up, "Would you tell the court what you mean by a move." "Well Your Honour, Your Worship, Sir, a move is turning over any two cards at the same time and you've got to use three moves. Wanna go?"

"His wig nearly dropped off. I assume it was a wig but no earrings." (Posh voice.) "Clerk, just demonstrate it for us."

"Don't bother, I'll show you."

(Think of them as 1, 2 and 3.)

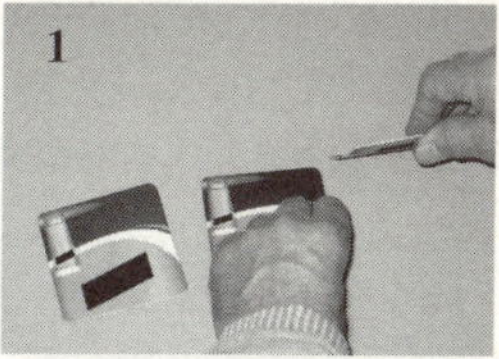

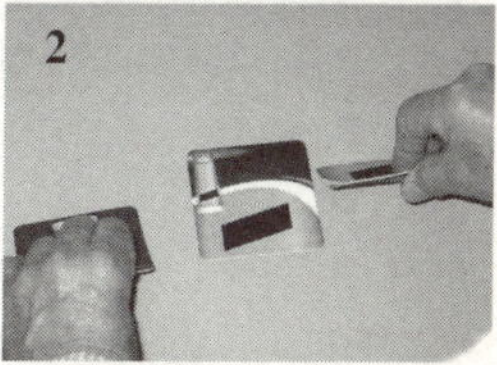

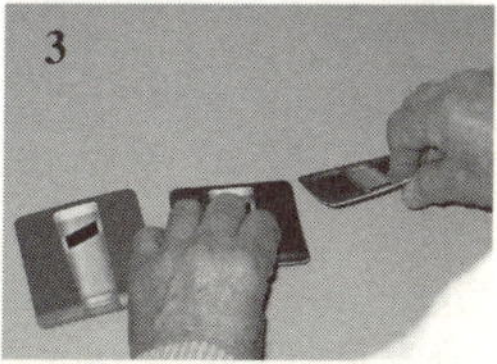

(Remember the moves as: 2 and 3,1 and 3,2 and 3 again. That's the way to do it, as shown to me by Ken.)

Immediately, turn the centre mat over and say, "Try it!"

"Remember 3 moves, a move is any 2 mats *at the same time*."

They won't manage it. Although it looks the same, it is in fact the exact opposite of *your* starting arrangement. If they have managed to duplicate your moves, it will look like this.

Say, "You're trying to *find* the lagers, not *down* them. I'll do it again." *Immediately* turn over the centre mat.

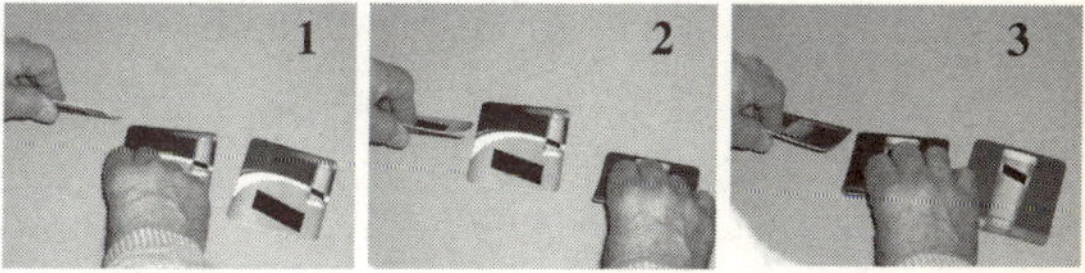

Do exactly the same moves again but this time, mentally, number the mats from the right.

Think: 2 and 3, 1 and 3, 2 and 3 again. It will look different to your audience but not to you. This time when you turn over the centre mat,

Say, "I'll show you how to do it. Think of them
as 1, 2 and 3. Then turn over, 2 and 3, 1 and 3, 2 and 3 again.

They won't manage it, of course. *Immediately* turn over the centre mat and do it successfully. You must use discretion with this one, you mustn't embarrass anyone with it. Keep the mood light and then start talking about the Find the Lady swindle.

Explain that it is still being used in London and elsewhere but instead of the traditional arrangement of two Jacks and a Queen, they are using mats.

One of the mats has little labels stuck on it and you have to bet on which one it is after, of course, they have been moved around a bit, face down. So the swindle is Find the *Label*. "Oh, no, Officer, I wouldn't dream of doing that old swindle Find the Lady. Look! There's no lady." Pathetic though it may seem, that's part of the logic behind the change but much more importantly, punters may be lulled into thinking that this is something different. It isn't.

My Card

The *Find the Lager* (p.44) challenge is extremely versatile since it can be done with almost anything that can be turned over or round: coins, cards, even tumblers. (Empty.)
In a commercial situation they can be an easy way of leaving your details, simply use your business cards then say, "Try it later. Get stuck, give me a ring."
As an example, my first card:

In a pulling situation you can use the same dodge but with different cards. If you've got access to a computer you can easily design and print your own. If not, ask round, pop into a cyber cafe, a library or quite probably a shopping or service centre. This sort of thing:

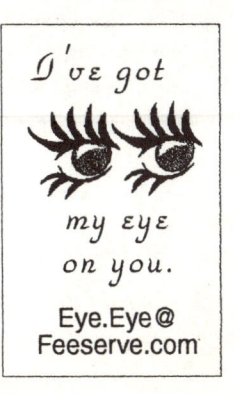

I've got
my eye on you.
Eye.Eye@Feeserve.com

Just call me Muscles.
Just call me.
0777 XXXX XXXX

Match It

Find the Lady is, of course, a scam, hundreds of years old but still catching the unwary always warn friends never to become involved, you cannot win and can end up with a broken rib. The following is a scam that my father showed me, age seven. No, *I* was seven. It fooled me then but, incredibly, it was still fooling punters on television only recently. You work it like this.

As with many scams it is all in the wording. It is an act - you must convince the punter that you are making a serious offer.

Empty out a match box and place a pound coin inside. Do everything very openly, slowly and deliberately. Close the box, rattle it and then *slowly* open the box. "No trickery. The pound is still there. If you are willing to match it by also putting a pound in the box.....

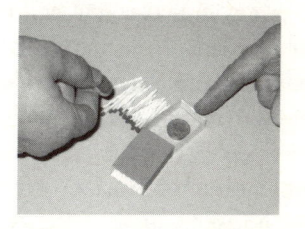

..... you can have the whole thing for £1.50." People do !!!

Finger Pricking Good!

Another age-old scam, Pricking the Garter, you can do it with a belt, tie, ribbon, tape measure or anything else that will fold easily into a *double* spiral. Note it is folded not quite at the middle so that when it is curled up, one end protrudes further than the other.

Two loops are formed at the centre. Ask someone to place his finger, or a ballpoint, etc., into the *true centre* of the tape. (Keep your eye on it.) How you uncurl the tape, can make him win (1) or lose (2) the bet.

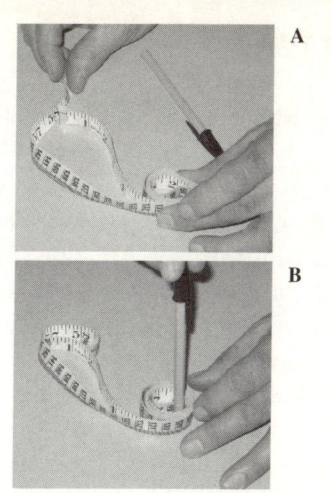

If he chooses the loosing loop, then unwind *both* ends together. If not, first wind the outer tape A round to position B and then unwind both ends together as before.

String Thing

Staying with loopy ideas, take out a piece of thin string, about 1.5m (say, 5 feet) long, tied in a loop. "Like to string along with me? Would you mind slipping your ring off, please but hold on to it *firmly*." Thread the loop through the ring and adjust her hold so she is gripping the edge of the ring tightly between her thumb and forefinger.

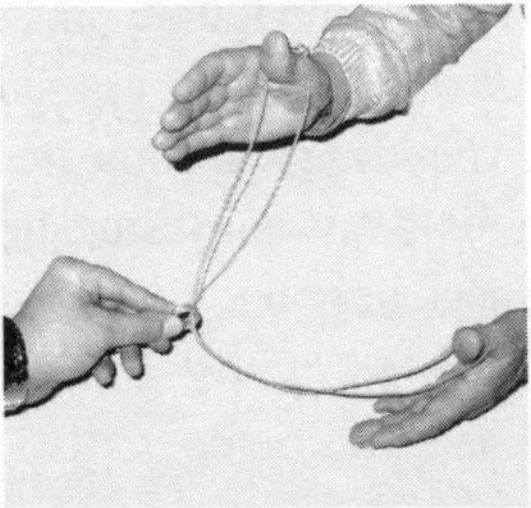

Bring your hands closer together and hook the string with your little fingers:

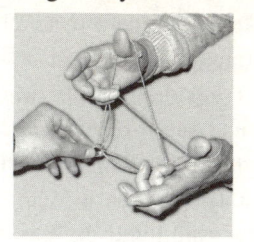

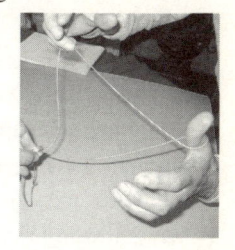

Slip the string off your *right* thumb and immediately bring the thumb and forefingers together on *both* your hands, gripping the ends of the loop. The string will come free. 'Snap it' twice to show that it is a complete loop and ask her to check her ring.

Sawing Thru'

String Thing (page 58) is extremely versatile and well worth perfecting until you don't have to think about it. Try penetrating the arm of a chair, or a person if wearing sleeves. "You've heard of Sawing thru' a Woman, well this is how it's done. This is the woman." Touch the arm lightly. "And this is the saw." 'Snap' the string loop. "You saw it before."

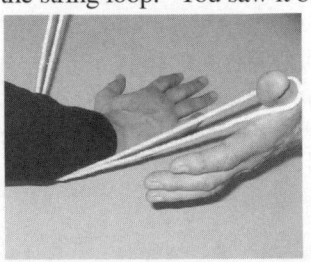

Slip the loop under the arm and do the 'ring thing' (p. 58).

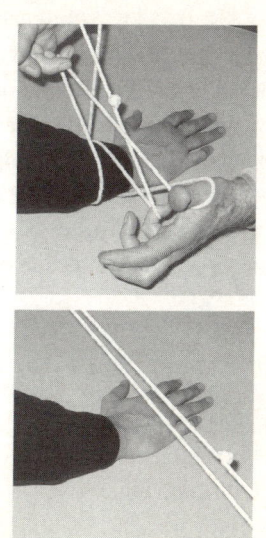

Lucky Number Lottery

Lotteries are big business, millions go in for them every week, some twice a week, so you predicting a freely chosen number on a lottery slip will always capture people's interest and, always remember, that's what pulling is about. You need two lottery slips and a scrap of paper or, ideally, your card (see pages 52-53). At the bottom of one of the slips, write in the following numbers:

[1] [2] [3] [4] [5] [6] [7] [8] [9] [10] [11] [12]
[13] [14] [15] [16] [17] [18] [19] [20] [21] [22] [23] [24]
[25] [26] [27] [28] [29] [30] [31] [32] [33] [34] [35] [36]
[37] [38] [39] [40] [41] [42] [43] [44] [45] [46] [47] [48]

Fold this section underneath so it is hidden and place it on top of the other lottery slip.

"The trouble with lotteries is there are too many numbers but the Lucky Number Lottery only uses a small square of them, 4 by 4, something like this."

[1] [2] [3] [4] [5] [6] [7] [8] [9] [10] [11] [12]
[13] [14] [15] [16] [17] [18] [19] [20] [21] [22] [23] [24]
[25] [26] [27] [28] [29] [30] [31] [32] [33] [34] [35] [36]
[37] [38] [39] [40] [41] [42] [43] [44] [45] [46] [47] [48]

Draw a sample on your slip then give her the other one and ask her to draw a 4 by 4 square anywhere along the top row.

Check that it *is* 4 by 4 then remember the top left corner number, in this example, 4. "I'm going to write down what I think is *your* Lucky Number but not to influence you, I'll turn away."

With your body hiding your writing, unfold the bottom section. As an example, let's suppose that her square began with the number 7, looking down that column on your slip gives a figure of 106. Fold the bottom section underneath so that it is again hidden. Print that number clearly on your slip of paper or your card and then fold it in half. Turn round and place it under her glass.

"In Lucky Lottery you are allowed *one* number from any row or column. Please ring any number in your square. Now strike out the rest in that row and that column."

```
[ 7 ] [ 8 ] [ 9̸ ] [10]
[19] [20] [(21)] [22]
[31] [32] [3̸3̸] [34]
[43] [44] [4̸5̸] [46]
```

"Do it again, please, with any number you haven't crossed out."

```
[ 7 ] [ 8 ] [ 9̸ ] [10]
[19] [20] [(21)] [22]
[31] [32] [3̸3̸] [34]
[43] [44] [4̸5̸] [46]
```

"And, please, once again. Any number you haven't already crossed out."

```
[ 7] [ 8] [ 9] [10]
[19] [20] [21] [22]
[31] [32] [33] [34]
[43] [44] [45] [46]
```

"Good, that. leaves one number you haven't crossed out, 46. So let's add up your four choices and see if they make your Lucky Number. Let's see, you chose 21, 8, 31 and 46. 21 and 8 are 29 and 31 are 60 and 46 makes 106. Now the Big Question, did you choose your Lucky Number? Would you please look at that paper where I wrote down your number before you ever started."

What do you do if, after someone has seen you do the trick, you are challenged, when you haven't got your 'crib' slip? Easy There are two ways of doing it. Add up the diagonal starting with the top left hand number, in this example, 7.

The diagonal is 7+20+33+46 =106.

Another way to do it, if you remember that the number 1 column carries the total of 82, simply add 4 for every column up to and including the chosen starter column, 7.

That is, 82+4+4+4+4+4+4 giving 106.

Use whichever method you find the easier but, whichever you choose, just take your time.

Bread Bun

You find money in your roll. Crumbs! Here are two ways of doing it to suit the situation. If attention is away from you, take out a small coin and hold the roll under the table. Press your thumb nail into the underside of the roll and press the coin into the slit. Place it on your side plate and wait for the right moment.

"Oh, I recognise this, it's what's known as a bread roll." When the attention is on you, press the ends of the roll *downwards*, breaking open the roll and disclosing the coin.

"There it is, the bread."

In other situations, secretly take out a coin and let it lie in your curled right fingers as you pick up the roll with your left.

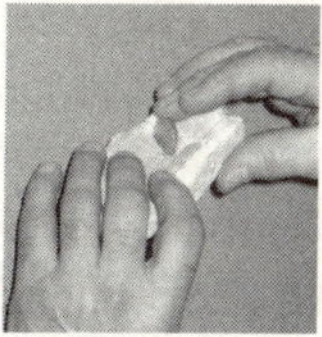

Press both ends of the roll *upwards* producing a crack underneath. Push coin into it.

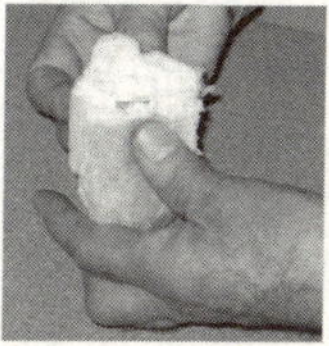

Push the ends of the roll *downwards*, breaking the roll so you can 'find' the coin.

Money *Mat*-ters

You can use essentially the same technique to find money in a drink mat. Secretly take out a bank note, folded to ⅛th size, hidden in your curled right fingers as you pick up a drinks mat with your left hand. Turn the mat over a few times and squeeze the centre.

"I think so, this could be one."
Bring the mat over the note so that it is hidden.

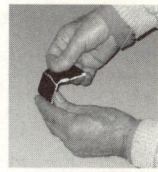

"They're all at it. Promotions."
Fold the mat *downwards* so that it breaks, concealing the note inside. *Slide* the note towards the inner right corner and fold the mat *downwards* into four.

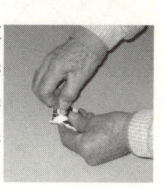

"I think......" Gradually pick away at the centre of the mat to reveal the note. "I thought so."

Blow Me

Pull the centre of a handkerchief or a napkin up through your left hand fingers.

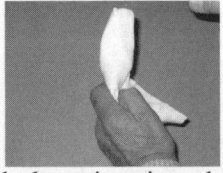

Lean over and take an imaginary hair from the girl's shoulder. "Nice." 'Wrap it' round the base of the handkerchief just above where your left thumb rests against it.

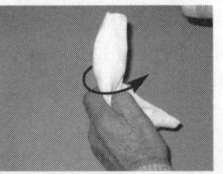

Apparently pull on the hair with your right hand as you secretly press with your left thumb against the cloth. Co-ordinate your movements correctly and it will look as though you are controlling it with the hair.

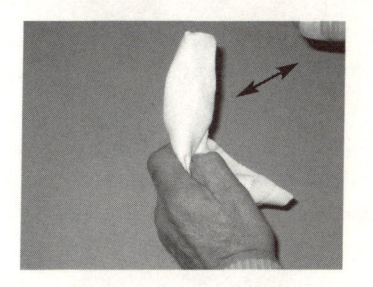

Unwind it and slip the hair onto your shoulder. "Thanks, it'll make a souvenir."

Jump!

Slip a small rubber band around the first two fingers of your left hand.

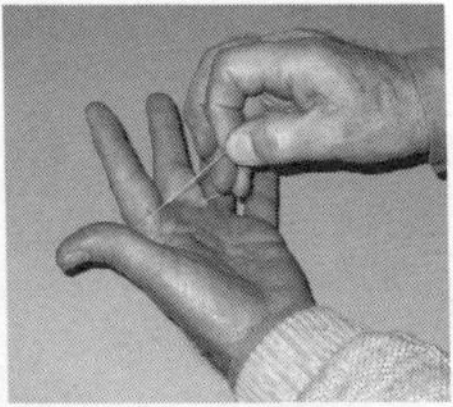

'Snap' it a few times with the thumb and forefinger of your right hand.

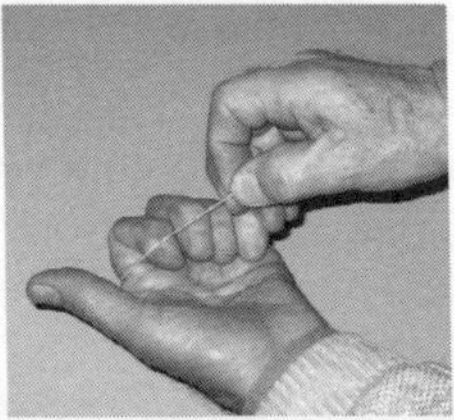

On the last snap, pull the band well out from your fingers so that *all your right fingers* go inside. Clench your left hand so that the band goes *across all four left finger nails.*

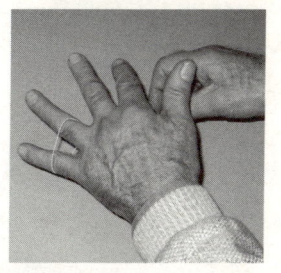

Make a snapping sound with your right hand. Say, *"Jump!"* Rapidly straighten your left fingers and the band *will* jump.

Beat the Band

Replace the band on the first two fingers of your *left* hand as you say, "You know, some people think it comes off your fingers on to the other ones. Ridiculous. I'll show you."

Take out a longer rubber band with your right hand.

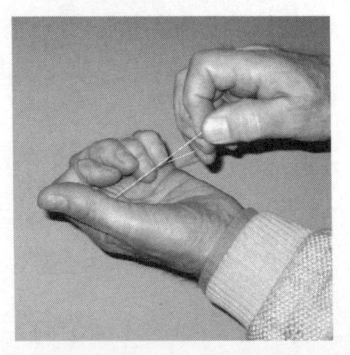

Loop the end of the longer band on to the tips of your *lefthand fingers*.

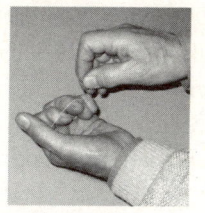

You then do *exactly* the same moves as before. You'll probably be surprised to find that the 'restraining' band does not make any difference at all!

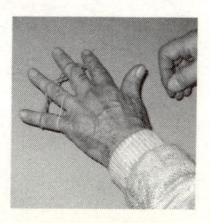

You're A Card!

Once you become known for doing magic, someone will ask you to do a card trick so it is best to be prepared and we will get to that a little later.(p.90)

What if you want to do some card magic but you are not yet known for it, how do you introduce the idea? One way is *not* to keep your cards in a box !

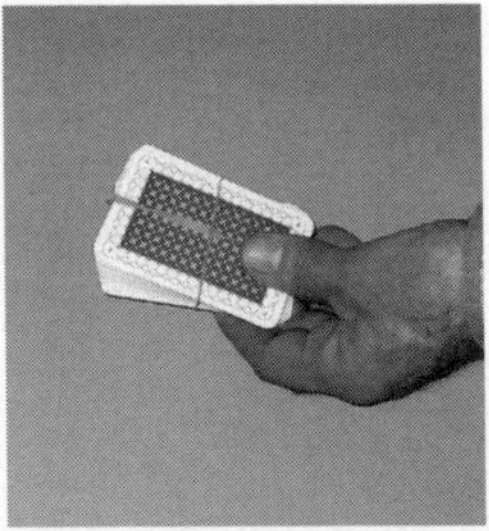

That's it, take off the rubber bands and make them 'Jump!' (page 74) Then say, "I saw a great puzzle the other day, you had to make a magic square with nine cards." Take out an ace to nine of any suits.

A♦, 2♥, 3♠, 4♣, 5♥, 6♣, 7♠, 8♣, 9♦.

Magic squares make an ideal 'opener' since everybody knows of them but relatively few know how to make one.

```
        6♣  A♦  8♣
        7♠  5♥  3♠
        2♥  9♦  4♠
```

All rows, columns and *both* diagonals add up to 15.

The good news is you don't have to *remember* it, you can easily work it out and use the technique to construct others. At the most, all you have to remember are the four cards; Ace, 2, 5 ,9. (Use any suits.)

$$
\begin{array}{ccc}
6\clubsuit & A\diamondsuit & 8\clubsuit \\
7\spadesuit & 5\heartsuit & 3\spadesuit \\
2\heartsuit & 9\diamondsuit & 4\spadesuit
\end{array}
$$

If you arrange the numbers 1 to 9 in pairs, each totalling 10: (1+9) +(2+8)+(3+7)+(4+6) + 5 it is easy to see that the total is 10+10+10+10+5 = 45.

The square has three rows so each row must total 45/3 =15.

So the Magic Constant is 15.

Look at the centre column. It starts with the lowest number and ends with the largest and in the middle, is the number that is halfway between the two: five.

The only other thing to remember is that the two goes in either the top or bottom row.

If I try to put it in the top row, 1+2=3 and taking 3 from 15 leaves 12 and we don't have a twelve, so it must go in the bottom row. (Either corner.)

The rest follows by adding pairs and subtracting from 15.

(Warning: only explain the method if you feel that the pullee would be interested in it!)

Happy Birthday

If there is an 18th birthday guy or gal about, try this:

$$7\clubsuit \quad 2\diamondsuit \quad 9\clubsuit$$
$$8\spadesuit \quad 6\heartsuit \quad 4\spadesuit$$
$$3\heartsuit \quad 10\diamondsuit \quad 5\spadesuit$$

Again, you don't have to *remember* it, you can work it out from the 15 square: all you do is add one to the value of each card, so you replace the ace by a two, the two by a three, and so on up to ten.

You can give it a 'romantic' look by using the two to ten of hearts to create it.

Similarly you can give it a money or wealth connotation by selecting the two to ten of diamonds, then saying, "Your future looks bright, look at all those diamonds," then remove the six from the centre.

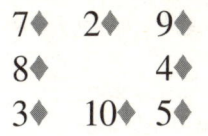

$$7♦ \quad 2♦ \quad 9♦$$
$$8♦ \quad \quad 4♦$$
$$3♦ \quad 10♦ \quad 5♦$$

"Oh, look a diamond ring. Makes you think." Similarly clubs and spades can be used to personalise the magic square if you can spot a suitable linking interest.

Pontoon Puzzler

This 'bar bet' works very well for players of card games such as pontoon, blackjack or 21 as actual card games or on slot machines, computers or the net.

The challenge is to use any nine cards from the pack (any suits) to make up a magic square in which all rows, columns and both diagonals add up to the winning total 21.

$$8\clubsuit \quad 3\diamondsuit \quad K\clubsuit$$
$$9\spadesuit \quad 7\heartsuit \quad 5\spadesuit$$
$$4\heartsuit \quad A\diamondsuit \quad 6\spadesuit$$

(4 individuals or groups can work on it at the same time.)

As with the Happy Birthday 18 square you don't have to remember it, you can construct it from the basic magic square of 15: 21-15 = 6. The 6 has to be divided over three numbers so the value of each card has to be increased by 2 giving the range 3 to 11.

What, of course, is nice about the bet is that it requires some basic knowledge of pontoon or blackjack. That is that a picture card counts ten and an ace can count as one or eleven.

Magic squares make a good talking point. The 15 square originated in ancient China as the *lo-shu*. Check with Google.

Blackjack Baffler

This is a great follow-up to the Pontoon Puzzler challenge/bet because, at first, it looks like just another magic square but it ain't. Lay out the 9 cards, any suits:

4	7	5
7	10	8
6	9	7

"I have a feeling you are just naturally lucky. I bet you could always get 21 at blackjack or pontoon. This is how it works, you're allowed one card from any row or column. I am sure you will end up with three cards that total 21, To start, which card would you like?"

Let's suppose that she chose the six of diamonds and we will follow it from there as an example.

In fact, it does not matter at all which card is chosen. The trick does work automatically as long as you follow the one basic rule of only one card from any one row or column.

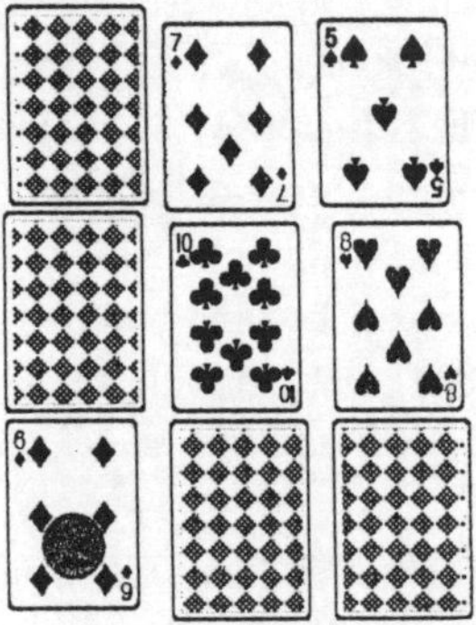

"OK, so you've chosen the six of diamonds. I'll place a coin on it to mark it and turn over the two other cards in the same row and column. Now, please, choose any other face-up card."

"You've chosen the seven of diamonds, so I'll mark it and turn over the other cards in same row and column. That leaves the 8 of hearts. So let's add the 3 cards: 6+7+8 makes 21 ! I knew you were lucky."

Show us a trick!

So now they know you do magic and it is OK to offer to do a trick. That hurdle is over but you need to be ready to be challenged at any time, by anybody, with any pack. "Show us a trick!"

Hand the pack to the challenger and ask him to shuffle the pack, as you take it back, tilt the pack *slightly* and note the bottom card.

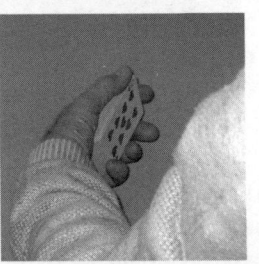

Place the pack on the table and ask him to cut it.

Immediately place the lower half *cross-wise* on top of the other half. Look straight at the challenger and say, "I'd like a number between one and ten!"

No matter what he says, call out, "Correct!" This gag is to misdirect his attention away from what you are going to do.

He will look baffled. "What card?" You didn't ask him to look at *any* card, never mind remember it. *You* pretend to be amazed. "You didn't look at your card' There's always one. Never mind, just remember it." Lift up the top half of the pack and show him the face card. Make sure he has seen it and others nearby. Replace the top half and square the pack.

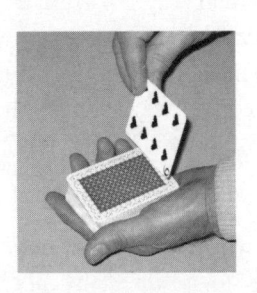

The card that he is being asked to remember is, of course, the bottom card that you noted after he had shuffled the pack. That little piece of play-acting is essential to the trick. Now you follow it with a little more of the same.

"Right, I'd like you to make your mind a perfect blank." Look absolutely amazed. "Why that's incredible! OK, just think of your card."

Pretend to have difficulties.

Ask him to make it easier by just thinking of the colour, red or black. Then just the suit, then high or low, and finally the complete card. Applause!

You Chose Your Card !

Exactly the same trick can be worked to 'force' a particularly relevant card on the pullee.

Look through the pack as you say, "We won't need the Jokers." Remove any but at the same time, secretly, cut the Queen of Hearts to the bottom of the pack. Place the pack on the table and ask her to cut it. Complete the cut with the bottom half placed *crosswise* and then proceed as before (page 91) but at the stage of revealing the whole card, say, "Oh, you've made it too easy for me, choosing your own card. The Queen of Hearts."

Jumping Jack

With a man do exactly the same but with the Jack of Clubs, finishing with the line, "I thought so, it's Jack the Lad, the Jack of Clubs." Place the Jack openly on top of the pack then *undercut* like this.

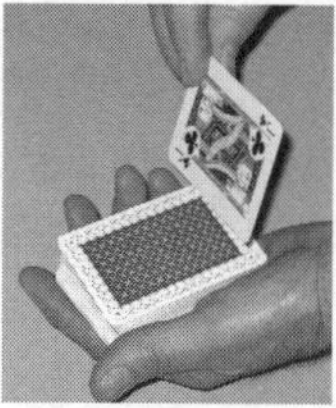

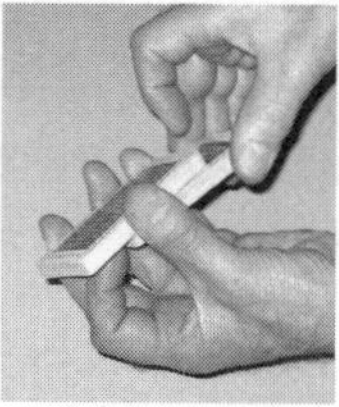

Slap the lower half on to the table and then *slap* the top half on top of it. Pick up the pack, flick the top card and turn it over. "He's a Jumping Jack !"

The Golden Rules of Magic

crystallize the actual performing experience of many thousands of magicians over hundreds of years.

1 Never tell how a trick is done.

The 'method' (how it is done) is never as amazing as the 'effect' (what the audience *thinks* they saw). That is the *magic* of magic.

2 Never repeat a trick to the same audience.

Repetition forces the audience to concentrate on the method, not on the effect, and the *magic* of magic is lost.

3 Practise! Practise! Practise!

Make sure you know what you are going to do and what you are going to say before a performance.

**Finally, remember, Have Fun,
and so will your audience.**